Greetings from
DAYTONA
BEACH
THE WORLD'S MOST FAMOUS BEACH
Florida

Greetings from
DAYTONA
BEACH
THE WORLD'S MOST FAMOUS BEACH
Florida

Greetings from
DAYTONA
BEACH
THE WORLD'S MOST FAMOUS BEACH
Florida

Greetings from
DAYTONA
BEACH
THE WORLD'S MOST FAMOUS BEACH
Florida

Greetings from
DAYTONA
BEACH
THE WORLD'S MOST FAMOUS BEACH
Florida

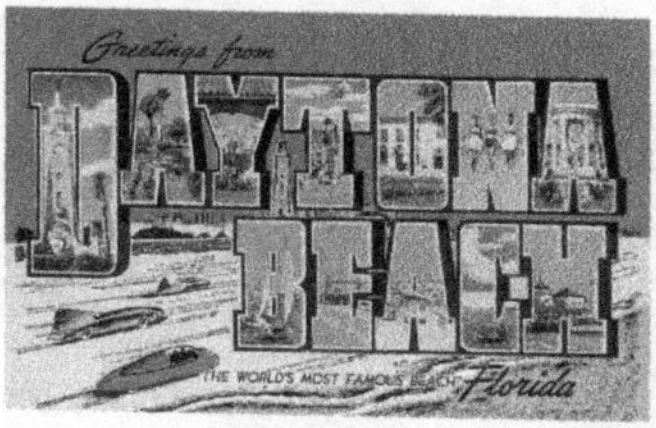
Greetings from
DAYTONA
BEACH
THE WORLD'S MOST FAMOUS BEACH
Florida

Greetings from
DAYTONA
BEACH
THE WORLD'S MOST FAMOUS BEACH
Florida

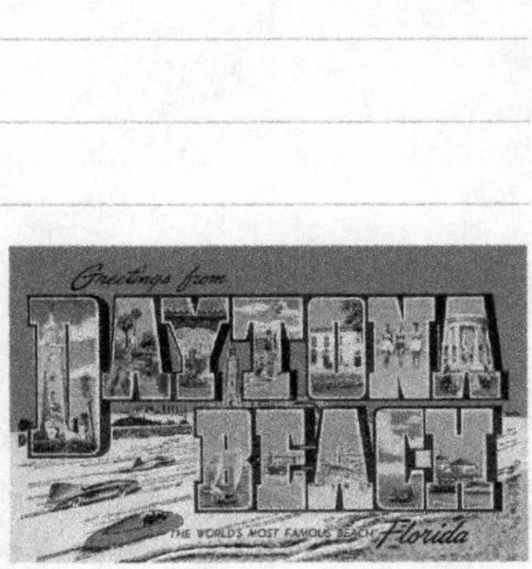
Greetings from
DAYTONA
BEACH
THE WORLD'S MOST FAMOUS BEACH
Florida

Greetings from
DAYTONA
BEACH
THE WORLD'S MOST FAMOUS BEACH
Florida

Greetings from
DAYTONA
BEACH
THE WORLD'S MOST FAMOUS BEACH
Florida

Greetings from
DAYTONA
BEACH
THE WORLD'S MOST FAMOUS BEACH
Florida

Greetings from
DAYTONA
BEACH
THE WORLD'S MOST FAMOUS BEACH
Florida

Greetings from
DAYTONA
BEACH
THE WORLD'S MOST FAMOUS BEACH
Florida

Greetings from
DAYTONA
BEACH
THE WORLD'S MOST FAMOUS
Florida

Greetings from
DAYTONA
BEACH
THE WORLD'S MOST FAMOUS BEACH
Florida

Greetings from
DAYTONA
BEACH
THE WORLD'S MOST FAMOUS BEACH
Florida

Greetings from
DAYTONA
BEACH
THE WORLD'S MOST FAMOUS BEACH
Florida

Greetings from
DAYTONA
BEACH
THE WORLD'S MOST FAMOUS BEACH
Florida

Greetings from
DAYTONA
BEACH
THE WORLD'S MOST FAMOUS BEACH
Florida

Greetings from
DAYTONA
BEACH
THE WORLD'S MOST FAMOUS BEACH
Florida

Greetings from
DAYTONA
BEACH
Florida

Greetings from
DAYTONA
BEACH
THE WORLD'S MOST FAMOUS
Florida

Greetings from
DAYTONA
BEACH
THE WORLD'S MOST FAMOUS BEACH
Florida

Greetings from
DAYTONA
BEACH
THE WORLD'S MOST FAMOUS
Florida

Greetings from
DAYTONA
BEACH
THE WORLD'S MOST FAMOUS BEACH
Florida

Greetings from
DAYTONA
BEACH
THE WORLD'S MOST FAMOUS
Florida

Greetings from
DAYTONA
BEACH
THE WORLD'S MOST FAMOUS
Florida

Greetings from
DAYTONA
BEACH
THE WORLD'S MOST FAMOUS BEACH
Florida

Greetings from
DAYTONA
BEACH
THE WORLD'S MOST FAMOUS BEACH
Florida

Greetings from
DAYTONA
BEACH
THE WORLD'S MOST FAMOUS BEACH
Florida

Greetings from
DAYTONA
BEACH
THE WORLD'S MOST FAMOUS BEACH
Florida

Greetings from
DAYTONA
BEACH
THE WORLD'S MOST FAMOUS BEACH
Florida

Greetings from
DAYTONA
BEACH
THE WORLD'S MOST FAMOUS BEACH
Florida

Greetings from
DAYTONA
BEACH
THE WORLD'S MOST FAMOUS BEACH
Florida

Greetings from
DAYTONA
BEACH
THE WORLD'S MOST FAMOUS BEACH
Florida

Greetings from
DAYTONA
BEACH
THE WORLD'S MOST FAMOUS BEACH
Florida

Greetings from
DAYTONA
BEACH
THE WORLD'S MOST FAMOUS BEACH
Florida

Greetings from
DAYTONA
BEACH
THE WORLD'S MOST FAMOUS BEACH
Florida

Greetings from
DAYTONA
BEACH
THE WORLD'S MOST FAMOUS BEACH
Florida

Greetings from
DAYTONA
BEACH
THE WORLD'S MOST FAMOUS BEACH
Florida

Greetings from
DAYTONA
BEACH
THE WORLD'S MOST FAMOUS BEACH
Florida

Greetings from
DAYTONA
BEACH
THE WORLD'S MOST FAMOUS BEACH
Florida

Greetings from
DAYTONA
BEACH
THE WORLD'S MOST FAMOUS BEACH
Florida

Greetings from
DAYTONA
BEACH
THE WORLD'S MOST FAMOUS BEACH
Florida

Greetings from
DAYTONA
BEACH
THE WORLD'S MOST FAMOUS
Florida

Greetings from
DAYTONA
BEACH
THE WORLD'S MOST FAMOUS BEACH
Florida

Greetings from
DAYTONA
BEACH
THE WORLD'S MOST FAMOUS BEACH
Florida

Greetings from
DAYTONA
BEACH
THE WORLD'S MOST FAMOUS
Florida

Greetings from
DAYTONA
BEACH
THE WORLD'S MOST FAMOUS BEACH
Florida

Greetings from
DAYTONA
BEACH
THE WORLD'S MOST FAMOUS BEACH
Florida

Greetings from
DAYTONA
BEACH
THE WORLD'S MOST FAMOUS BEACH
Florida

Greetings from
DAYTONA
BEACH
THE WORLD'S MOST FAMOUS BEACH
Florida

Greetings from
DAYTONA
BEACH
THE WORLD'S MOST FAMOUS BEACH
Florida

Greetings from
DAYTONA
BEACH
THE WORLD'S MOST FAMOUS BEACH
Florida

Greetings from
DAYTONA
BEACH
THE WORLD'S MOST FAMOUS BEACH
Florida

Greetings from
DAYTONA
BEACH
THE WORLD'S MOST FAMOUS BEACH
Florida

Greetings from
DAYTONA
BEACH
THE WORLD'S MOST FAMOUS BEACH
Florida

Greetings from
DAYTONA
BEACH
THE WORLD'S MOST FAMOUS BEACH
Florida

Greetings from
DAYTONA
BEACH
THE WORLD'S MOST FAMOUS BEACH
Florida

Greetings from
DAYTONA
BEACH
THE WORLD'S MOST FAMOUS
Florida

Greetings from
DAYTONA
BEACH
THE WORLD'S MOST FAMOUS BEACH
Florida

Greetings from
DAYTONA
BEACH
THE WORLD'S MOST FAMOUS BEACH
Florida

Greetings from
DAYTONA
BEACH
THE WORLD'S MOST FAMOUS BEACH
Florida

Greetings from
DAYTONA
BEACH
THE WORLD'S MOST FAMOUS BEACH
Florida

Greetings from
DAYTONA
BEACH
THE WORLD'S MOST FAMOUS BEACH
Florida

Greetings from
DAYTONA
BEACH
THE WORLD'S MOST FAMOUS BEACH
Florida

Greetings from
DAYTONA
BEACH
Florida

Greetings from
DAYTONA
BEACH
THE WORLD'S MOST FAMOUS BEACH
Florida

Greetings from
DAYTONA
BEACH
THE WORLD'S MOST FAMOUS
Florida

Greetings from
DAYTONA
BEACH
THE WORLD'S MOST FAMOUS BEACH
Florida

Greetings from
DAYTONA
BEACH
THE WORLD'S MOST FAMOUS BEACH
Florida

Greetings from
DAYTONA
BEACH
THE WORLD'S MOST FAMOUS BEACH
Florida

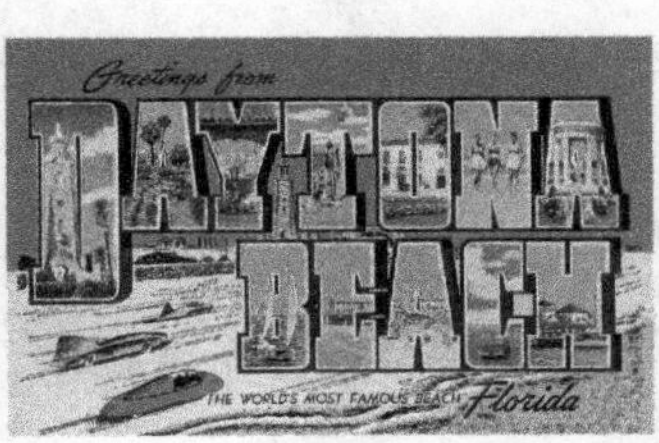
Greetings from
DAYTONA
BEACH
THE WORLD'S MOST FAMOUS BEACH
Florida

Greetings from
DAYTONA
BEACH
"THE WORLD'S MOST FAMOUS BEACH"
Florida

Greetings from
DAYTONA
BEACH
Florida

Printed in the USA
CPSIA information can be obtained
at www.ICGtesting.com
LVHW092306210724
785953LV00014B/39

9 798385 408160